THE MINISTRY OF CONSOLATION

The Ministry of Consolation

A Parish Guide for Comforting the Bereaved

REV. TERENCE P. CURLEY, D.Min.

ALBA · HOUSE   N E W · Y O R K
SOCIETY OF ST. PAUL, 2187 VICTORY BLVD., STATEN ISLAND, NY 10314

Library of Congress Cataloging-in-Publication Data

Curley, Terence P., 1944-
    The ministry of consolation : the parish guide for comforting
the bereaved / Terence P. Curley.
        p.   cm.
    Includes bibliographical references.
    ISBN 0-8189-0651-0
    1. Catholic Church. Order of Christian funerals. 2. Church
work with the bereaved. 3. Catholic Church — Clergy. 4. Catholic
Church — Membership.   I. Title.
BX2035.6.F8523C873   1993   93-10315
259'.6 — dc20   CIP

Produced and desinged in the United States of
America by the Fathers and Brothers of the
Society of St. Paul, 2187 Victory Boulevard,
Staten Island, New York 10314, as part of their
communications apostolate.

PRINTING INFORMATION:

Current Printing - first digit 1 2 3 4 5 6 7 8 9 10 11 12

Year of Current Printing - first year shown
1993   1994   1995   1996   1997   1998   1999   2000

Dedication

To
my Aunt,
Mary E. Koen
May she enjoy
the
Peace of the Kingdom.

Preface

The parish is the place for the bereaved to express the many feelings which accompany separation and loss. Since the promulgation of the new *Order of Christian Funerals* more attention is being focused on the needs of the bereaved.

The new ritual emphasizes the importance of participation and ministry in all of the rites of Christian burial. Along with this the ritual stresses the presence of the community. The parish journeys with the deceased during the final liturgies. During this journey a covenant is establish with the bereaved. The ministry of consolation entails being sensitive toward those who are grief-stricken.

Rituals facilitate grief. They are healing agents for those who must express their losses. The parish, with its many caregivers, can help the bereaved to ritualize their losses.

This work connects the new ritual to the reality of pastoral care, from the time for the funeral through the whole process of bereavement. It also highlights the need for the community to reach out to the bereaved through a pastoral visiting program. Pastoral visitors are often the most effective caregivers in assisting the bereaved.

The underlying theme of this work is the need to connect with the community of faith at critical times. The death of a Christian affects the entire parish. Working together to assist the bereaved transforms the parish community, as compassion and caring take on a flesh and blood presence. This book is written with the wish that we will become more hopeful as we journey and express ourselves together as Christ's Body, and empowered by his presence.

Contents

1. Comforting the Bereaved 1

2. The New Ritual: A Better Connection 4

3. Grief Through the Eyes of A Child 11

4. Initiating a Pastoral Visiting Ministry 18

5. Funeral Homilies as Pastoral Care 25

6. Saying Farewell at the Funeral Liturgy 31

7. Psalms for Separation and Loss 39

8. Music Expressing Pastoral Care 45

9. Family Prayers During Bereavement and Beyond ... 53

10. Ritualizing Our Losses 60

11. Developing a Theology of Bereavement 64

Bibliography 71

1.

Comforting the Bereaved

What do Hansel and Gretel, Cinderella, Snow White, and Bambi have in common? They all suffered the loss of a parent. Some of these stories begin with a parent's death making the wicked stepmother the evil character.

Through history fairy tales have illustrated that life is not always carefree. Bad things happen, and we suffer. I recently asked my six year old niece how she felt when Bambi's mother died. She replied, "My eyes filled up." It was encouraging that she was able to express her feelings about a very real loss.

Living with separation and loss means being aware of our feelings. Expressing grief is no easy task for us. It takes time and the right setting to work it through.

All of us need to develop consoling ways to deal with losses. Unfortunately, many of us do this in a faulty way. Inappropriate statements and judgments are made with the bereaved. Even destructive advice is innocently offered.

It is possible to console others. We can help each other to manage losses rather than be controlled by them. Reaching out and touching the bereaved means being aware of what is needed in their lives. Checking on our way of communicating is vital if we are to be effective.

Comforting friends and others is something we can all do. Untold good is accomplished when we respond in a consoling way. More and more Catholics are being called to the ministry of consolation. You are needed to bring strength to others in your parish.

Hopefully, this knowledge will help us to be a little more self-confident and consoling as we minister to those who are experiencing the sadness of separation and loss. Very often the only consolation the bereaved experience is what friends offer. The more we are aware of the needs facing those who are grieving, the more effective we are for them.

Studies in crisis intervention emphasize the importance of being with the bereaved as soon as possible, that is, in the immediate time surrounding the death. Our presence is in itself a reassurance that others care. The shock and numbness may be lessened by supporting family and friends.

The real meaning of the ministry of consolation is expressed when parishioners respond in a loving way to the bereaved. Ministry may entail everything from picking up relatives at an airport to baby sitting or house sitting during the time of the funeral.

The bereaved receive comfort when they are allowed the freedom to express how they feel. Preparing the liturgy is vital, as the funeral rituals orient the bereaved to accept the loss. The pastoral caregiver is a key person in helping the bereaved to participate in the rituals of Christian burial. Even though it is painful, the more the loss is ritualized, the better the grief will be managed.

SOME IDEAS TO KEEP IN MIND . . .

* Helping the grieving means being physically there as soon as possible. The comforting presence is more significant than words.

* Don't offer platitudes. "It is all for the best." "It's God's will." They are not ready to hear that, no matter how well intentioned.

* Show empathy. Put yourself in the other person's position. "It must hurt you very much." "It must be a shock for you."

* Don't be afraid to touch or embrace the bereaved. Comfort happens with human contact.

* Offer to help with activities of daily life. This includes everything from shopping, picking people up at the airport, to baby sitting.

* Reassure the bereaved. As time goes by, help them to face their losses. You may mention a hospital or church support group.

* Help them to put the loss in the wider context of religious meaning. You may accompany them to religious services.

* Become more familiar with the process of grieving.

* Be patient. Don't expect instant results from your help. There is no time limit for grief work.

* Permit the bereaved to express their feelings of anger, abandonment, guilt, and yearning to be with the deceased.

* Keep in contact.

The new *Order of Christian Funerals* provides us with an effective emphasis for our appreciation of Christian death. We pray not only for the deceased but also for those bereaved who await the consolation of the Kingdom. The emphasis on the needs of the bereaved especially at the time of the funeral is a fine connection between liturgy and pastoral care. When we approach our grief and the new ritual in a creative way, we can go through the darkness of grief. Not only do we journey through the valley, but we do so in a way which converts our grief into gift.

Our grief is gift when the love of God is expressed by loving members of the Christian community. Hope communicates through the many rituals of kindness and love from a community which covenants to care for their grief-stricken members. The more we as Christians can facilitate the grieving process, the more consoling we are as parish families.

2.

The New Ritual — A Better Connection

On November 2, 1989 the new *Order of Christian Funerals* was implemented for parishes thoughout the United States. This long awaited revision of the 1969 rite will have far reaching consequences for American parish life. The most notable change is a complete shift in the focus of the rite. Formerly, the emphasis was on the mechanics of the rite and the priest's prayer options. Now it is on collaboration in the parish. The rite urges priests, deacons, pastoral associates, musicians, funeral directors and all parishioners to truly become ministers to the bereaved, in a collaborative effort that grows from the care of the community. The community is called to not only bury their dead but to minister to those left burdened by the loss.

As professionals, as parishioners and as caring people, we should ask a series of questions. Is the parish community aware of the collaborative perspective of the rite? Has the parish developed a ministry of consolation which meets the needs of the bereaved? Is there a realization that there is a connection between the ritual and pastoral care? In an effort to clarify these questions I will present examples of how they may be answered in the affirmative. Evaluation of the new rite's pastoral effectiveness depends on how the community ministers to the needs of the bereaved.

THE MINISTERING COMMUNITY

The new rite provides for a greater degree of involvement by the parish community. This means that the parish has to establish ways to allow its members to minister at liturgical and pastoral moments for the bereaved. What were thought to be special tasks of the clergy have to be reinterpreted.

There are significant times when instructed laity offer prayers — at the time of death, the gathering in the presence of the body, and the transfer of the deceased Christian to the Church or place of burial. The entire purpose of these additional prayers is to emphasize the Christian's journey as a member of the community. It is only fitting that brothers and sisters in Christ express this relationship to the deceased member. Support and comfort is extended to the bereaved at the same time.

A bereavement team or committee has to be established. There are many competent people who can assist in caring for the bereaved. The committee at first may need to be educated in pastoral care. Meetings can focus on information about the effects of grieving, how to adjust to losses, how to remember the loved one in the context of Christian faith and a spirituality of companions, how to help prepare liturgies and be supportive. The ways to assist include everything from picking up relatives at the airport to dropping off food for the bereaved family.

Whew we talk about the need to minister among ourselves as a community, we don't always provide ways to do so. The ministry of consolation can be spiritually enriching both for the bereaved and for the pastoral caregiver. Empathy and compassion are the necessary qualifications. This means being willing to be with others in their suffering.

Lent can be a special time for the committee to sponsor workshops to familiarize the parish with the new ritual. As we focus on preparation for the Resurrection, such considerations lend a more spiritual context to our own preparations.

Creative approaches, such as preplanning the funeral liturgy can be offered. If we are going to write wills, why not include instructions about the funeral liturgy? Preplanning should be an essential element to provide a prayerful celebration. This can be a hopeful rather than fearful experience for the Christian.

When parishioners gather together to prepare funeral liturgies, a change of attitude about death can happen. The preplanning reminds the Christian of his/her own mortality and the hope for immortality. The ritual's prayers and images assist us with a deeper appreciation of our spiritual journey toward the Kingdom of God.

An additional feature of preplanning funeral liturgies is the way it implements the new *Order of Christian Funerals*. The lector, musician, Eucharist Ministers, pastoral caregivers for the bereaved, parish support group, and parish bereavement committee are put into focus. In many ways preplanning is a communal rather than an individual endeavor.

MEETING THE NEEDS OF THE BEREAVED

The ministry of consolation has to accompany the funeral liturgies. The experience of loss can be a shattering time for the bereaved. When caregivers reach out and are present from the beginning, the grief-stricken are helped in accepting and managing the loss.

Pastoral visits to the bereaved, especially during the first year, illustrate the community's loving presence. The visits are important during this first year, as the intensity of remembering the loved one is felt at certain times. Anniversaries and holidays have a real effect. While they memorialize happy times they also intensify the feelings of loss, and scars thought to be healed break open again. Despite the inclination to be alone, the offering of someone being present at those times can do untold good.

The parish caring group can be of help to anyone experiencing the death of a loved one. It does not necessarily have to be a recent death. Current research about grief shows that there is no time limit for grieving. To the widow who needs practical help in adjusting her life, the caring group can provide help with everything from nutritional awareness to talking to grandchildren about death.

The group may meet in the rectory parlor every other week to discuss a variety of topics. The topics at first may relate to the symptoms of grief: the disorientation, anger, feelings of abandonment, yearning to be with the loved one, and ways of remembering.

Some typical pastoral examples demonstrate the need to have a grief support group in the parish:

Helen recently joined the caring group. She said that since she became a widow everything has been confused. The places she used to go with her husband are no longer happy for her. Yet, she finds that she is continually going back to places they used to frequent.

John's brother died out of state. Due to the distance and financial difficulties the body was cremated. The remains were returned home. John said that his mother was very upset when the ashes arrived. When the committal service was held the deceased's mother stated: "Eveything seemed very incomplete up until now."

Mary, a new member of the caring group, is an elderly widow who has experienced many losses. The most recent and devastating was the sudden death of her son while they were on vacation. She has problems praying. "I just don't have the right words to talk to God just now."

There is some very good literature about support groups available at this time. Creative ministry means being able to listen to the needs of the group and responding with supportive and timely topics. The facilitators are key people for the parish caring group. Often they are members of the parish bereavement committee. Parishioners who are counselors, nurses, lawyers, social workers, and others are frequently willing to facilitate the group.

THE RITUAL AND PASTORAL CARE

The new *Order of Christian Funerals* is a resource for pastoral care. It provides ways for the community to minister to the bereaved from the moment of the death. Prayers are offered with their family and friends at critical moments in the last journey for the deceased. The loss is placed into the wider context of religious meaning. This is the introduction to the grieving process which the bereaved have to go through as they mourn the death of a loved one.

There are many personal dimensions offered in the new ritual. It offers the family ways to remember the loved one by participating in the placing of symbols such as the pall or a family crucifix on the casket, reading religious remembrances at the time of final farewell, choosing readings and hymns, and being invited to bring up the gifts to the altar. What is very important is to include the bereaved in the new ritual which offers prayers for the bereaved family. The ritual also expresses the sadness which may be present among the mourners. Real hope is provided for the bereaved when they are able to release their feelings of loss at the liturgical moments.

The ongoing expression of grief can be done in the Christian community. Memorial Masses can help the bereaved express their loss in a way which can bring healing. One example of the connection between ritual and the reality of loss is clearly evident in the following pastoral example:

> Joan's infant son died three days after he was born. This was a
> shattering experience for Joan who was not married. She felt
> angry and abandoned in her grief. This happened three years
> ago. For the past two years she has requested that a memorial

Mass be offered on the anniversary. Joan's family has been supportive. The priest met with Joan a number of times. Recently, Joan arrived at a parish baptism for a friend's infant. At the time, the priest talked with her and she noted how difficult it was for her to attend. When the anniversary Mass was again offered, Joan quietly cried thoughout the liturgy. After the Mass, she offered the priest the customary offering. He refused the stipend and told Joan to buy something for her friend's baby. Joan looked pleased to be able to do this. She even said that the small present would be from her and in memory of her child Michael who had died.

Coping and spiritual growth in grief can go together. In this instance, Joan found a way to express her losses in the parish community. The ministry of consolation has to speak to the needs of the bereaved. The liturgy connects in many ways to the way grief may be expressed in a spiritually healthy way.

Our evaluation of the new ritual has to consider how the community is ministering to the bereaved through pastoral visits, caring groups, and liturgies which express hope and new ways of coping. We must be aware of the connection between what is done in liturgical gesture and action, and how that is fulfilled in pastoral care in the parish community.

It is not easy to implement the new *Order of Christian Funerals*. It is a challenge which has resurrectional results as it helps the grief-stricken to cope and see that from the darkness is the dawn of new life. The ministry helps the bereaved to live, trust, and take the risk of loving again.

3.

Grief Through The Eyes
Of A Child

The new *Order of Christian Funerals* highlights minstry and participation. The ritual's intention is liturgical involvement of all age groups at the time of the funeral and beyond.

Pastoral caregivers are familiar with many aspects of grief. When a child dies we direct our attention toward the grief-stricken parents, but this does not suffice. when death occurs we must focus on the entire family. We have to remember that siblings and children are just as much family members as the adults.

The pastoral caregiver is not always aware of how to go about working with children. Some important questions about children often arise at the time of the funeral. How we respond to children's participation affects in many ways the management and outcome of grief.

The question as to who should talk with a child about death is one of the most prevalent difficulties facing families. Very often adults too readily hand it over to the priest or pastoral caregiver. In light of modern insights to grief, it is necessary that we be prepared. Unfortunately, harm can be done if we are not sensitive to ways of communicating with children about death.

Recently, I visited the home of parishioners who were experiencing grief. The couple were middle-aged with three children aged nineteen, fourteen, and eight years. The maternal grandmother died rather suddenly after only a short stay in the hospital. I knew the family rather well as they are active in parish programs. When I arrived the wife was tearful as was her husband. While we were talking in the parlor, eight-year-old Danny came in and out of the room. He was playing with toys as usual and keeping busy.

The adult conversation was about grandmother's congestive heart failure and the complications leading to her death. The daughter is a nurse who had worked in cardiac care units. The conversation recounted her feelings and the differences she expeienced in having her mother as a patient. During the conversation events and personality characteristics about her deceased mother were recalled. She stated that, even though middle-aged, she felt like an "abandoned child" or "lost."

Eventually our conversation turned toward Danny. The mother's concern was that he wasn't crying. Danny tried to comfort his mother by telling her that she would be all right. He innocently said, "It really is not the end of the world." The remark was taken as comforting by his mother. She was aware that he meant well.

While she spoke I recalled my own nephew's remarks when my father died. Benjamin was only about five. He talked about my father to his grandmother, referring to him as "that man who used to live here." My nephew, like Danny, was close to his grandparents. Very young children are aware of adults' pain. Somehow children develop ways of talking which they believe lessen the painful recollections for adults. They in their own way try to comfort those whom they see suffering.

I asked Danny's mother if she had explained to her son what had happened to his grandmother. We talked a little about the child's need to feel included and to know what happened. In our conversation I explained that making known the medical causes often helps the child to accept the loss.

When Danny came back into the room, his mother asked him to sit down with us. She explained that his grandmother's heart was old and sick. "The heart stopped and Nana died. She didn't feel any pain." She went on to explain that everyone was sad because they missed Nana.

Danny listened and asked only a few questions about the hospital. He volunteered the information that he really didn't know what had happened. It was very fitting that Danny's mother would talk to him about the death. I was pleased and somewhat relieved that she decided to do this.

The next day was Sunday and according to custom I go to the local coffee shop in between Masses. It is a good time to meet informally with parishioners. The bereaved family happened to be at the shop. I spoke with the wife and she told me what happened. Shortly after I left, she had heard Danny crying in the other room. He had finished drawing three pictures. The first was of him with his grandmother. The second was of himself alone with the caption, "I love Nana." The third was of himself as a small figure (compared to the other pictures) all by himself.

The pictures provided a focus for the family. They were placed on the refrigerator door. Danny's pictures helped him and his family to express their loss. This incident demonstrates the need to relate to the child.

Children undergo grief in similar ways as do adults. What we ought to be aware of are the characteristics peculiar to children at their respective stages in development. Children react to death in ways appropriate to age. Like adults, they experience intense grief.

We cannot overestimate the importance of relating to the grieving child. Studies indicate that when a person is unable to complete the mourning tasks from childhood, they suffer later. Grief ministry means helping all age groups manage and resolve losses for the person's well-being. When we minister to children we need to keep in mind what the child is capable of understanding. How the child perceives the loss is another point to consider.

There is the need to give the child "permission" to grieve. The child's inner feelings may not be indicated by external behavior. It is not uncommon for children to express how they feel through play, acting out behaviors, or artistic creation.

We should expect some "magical thinking" by the child. This occurs when a child misinterprets reality and feels guilt that he or she did something that caused the person's death. This may have been not sending a thank-you note for a past gift or not giving a goodbye kiss. It is important to realize this and be clear cut with children about the physical causes of death.

Our language is important in the way we talk about death with the child. They can easily misinterpret our abstractions. For example, telling a child that someone was so good that God took them could bring about real problems. In the child's view this could mean that if you're really good God is going to take you too. This can be frightening and certainly shapes the child's image of God.

The child is searching for causes of the death. Sometimes we treat death the way we do questions about sexuality. The complex answer was really what the child was not wondering about. The way Danny's mother talked to him was helpful: she explained the causes clearly, simply and correctly.

Confusion occurs when the child isn't clear about causes. Another example is when we say someone "went away" or "is asleep." The child interprets this in a literal way. Such euphemisms only create problems. It is only natural for the child to wonder how to wake up the loved one. Or, if someone "went away" why did he/she abandon them? Was the child bad, which caused the deceased relative to leave?

Children often lack the opportunity to express feelings about losses — especially death. The adult has to be authentic and open in relating to the child. If we do not know answers we should simply be honest and tell the child. In other words our own feelings ought to be expressed. Death has to be related to the child's experience of loss. The death of a pet, a broken toy (which cannot be fixed) point toward the reality of loss.

The parish is the appropriate setting for ritualizing memories for children. Parish liturgies and religious education classes have to address the needs of bereaved children.

A parent's meeting can be held for liturgy preparation for specific age groups of children. Such a meeting helps to communicate the importance of remembering. Children are encouraged to remember and to pray for deceased relatives and friends in ways they can understand. The meeting helps everyone to be more aware of the need to express grief. It also activates our beliefs as Resurrectional People in eternal life.

Liturgical preparation can be done by the parish bereavement committee. It is a time to educate parents as well as children. The discussion can be invaluable in helping people sort out feelings and find deep religious meaning in the death of a loved one. For children in primary grades, the preparation may involve drawings of the family. This may even include great-grandparents. At their age the concept of ancestors can be learned through stories. Another experience may be directed toward parents. They may relate stories of parents, aunts, uncles they knew when they were the child's age. The adult child who perhaps was not provided with ways to grieve may be helped.

If children recall a deceased relative or friend, they may draw pictures. These pictures can later be put in church for the All Soul's Masses.

It ought to be noted that rituals help to resolve, channel, and manage our losses. The following outline of a prayer service is meant to help model what parishes can do for children and grief.

A CHILDREN'S PRAYER SERVICE FOR
THE DEATH OF LOVED ONES

Opening Hymn

Priest: The Grace and Peace of Jesus be with you all.

Response: And also with you.

Opening Prayer: Father, we have come together to remember
our loved ones who have died. We ask you to help us
pray for the souls of our grandmothers, grandfathers,
uncles, aunts, and for some mothers, fathers, and
brothers and sisters. Let us each pause for a moment and
remember our own loved ones. Help us to remember
them and give them your peace and love in heaven. We
ask this through Jesus Our Lord and Brother.   Amen.

First Reading: First Letter of John 3:1-2.

Psalm 23 (Sung).

Gospel: Mark 10:13-16.

Homily

Prayers of the Faithful: (Specific prayers developed at the liturgy
preparation session or at religious education periods may be
offered up with an age appropriate prayer by the child.)

Time for Reflection: (The priest may encourage children to say
what they remember or how they miss their loved ones. The
child may comment on the drawing and the message they
wish to convey about the deceased grandparent, sibling,
parent or others.)

Priest: The Peace of Christ be with you.
(At this time the priest may encourage the congregation to
offer each other some signs of hope or consolation)

Final Prayer & Closing Hymn.

4.

Initiating A Pastoral Visiting Ministry

Parishes are initiating new and more effective ways to minister to the bereaved, using the new *Order of Christian Funerals*. Reaching out and caring is the ministry of consolation which is of paramount importance according to the new ritual. The ritual calls the parish community to respond to the bereaved's needs through pastoral ministry.

A cornerstone for the ministry of consolation is the encounter between the bereaved and the caring community in the pastoral visit, whether it be at the time of the funeral or later in the grieving process. The parish initiates this ministry to bring comfort to those who are suffering losses. Not only do the bereaved receive spiritual help but the designated visitor does so too. Grief ministry can be an enriching pastoral experience for everyone.

Training is necessary for those who visit the bereaved. When the pastoral volunteer goes through some sessions he/she can be far more effective in caring and consoling. This chapter presents an overview of pastoral care in visiting the bereaved, a sketch of what we have to remember during training sessions for visitors.

PREPARING FOR PASTORAL VISITOR'S TRAINING

Ideally, a parish realizing the need for a consolation ministry will already have formed a bereavement committee. Such a committee generally acts as sponsor for pastoral activities regarding grief and loss. It consists of the parish staff and parish volunteers who want to participate in this important ministry.

The parish leadership designates a subcommittee of the parish bereavement committee. If a bereavement committee does not exist, then a subcommittee of the Parish Council may be formed. The subcommittee serves as a preparing or planning team for training parish visitors. From three to five sessions ought to be scheduled for the subcommittee.

It is necessary for the subcommittee to become familiar with ways to console those who are grieving. The leadership ought to look to some licensed mental health professional for assistance. Often there is such a person on the committee.

The subcommittee should outline three to five training sessions for the visitors. The visitors need to become familiar with ways to console and with the phases of grief.

VARIOUS PASTORAL VISITS

The overall intention is that the parish journeys with the bereaved through the phases of grief. Awareness as to what is happening in a grief-stricken person's life is a primary concern for visitors. The pastoral visits require different approaches depending upon timing and circumstances.

Often a parish minister will make initial contact with a family when visiting a critically ill person. This visit frequently happens while the parishioner is in the hospital or is connected with a hospice program.

When the pastoral visitor visits, it is advisable to make an effort to see the family in the hospital. This contact helps the parish visitor to establish a rapport. At this time the visitor may encounter anticipatory grief among family members. It is important that the visitor does not foster denial by insisting on hope in the face of impending death.

Pastoral assessments are made when the initial visit happens after the death of the loved one. The visitor may notice the intensity of feelings relating to the death. Often it is evident that the family is engaged in denial.

The pre-funeral visit happens when the parish hears about a death. This visit is meant to be practical and freeing for the bereaved. The loss of a loved one is a time of turmoil for the family. They need someone to assist them with the many details which they have to attend to.

> Members of the community should console the mourners with words of faith and support and with acts of kindness, for example, assisting them with some of the routine tasks of daily living. Such assistance may allow members of the family to devote time to planning the funeral rites with the priest and other ministers and may give the family time for prayer and mutual comfort.   *Order of Christian Funerals* (par. 10).

Pastoral visitors help with everything from house sitting during the funeral to picking up guests at the airport. These actions of love and concern demonstrate innate goodness and kindness.

About two weeks after the funeral, another pastoral visit takes place. Relatives have gone home and friends have returned to work. It is a time of loneliness for those left alone. The grieving process is still in its initial phase, characterized by shock and numbness. Along with these primary symptoms the bereaved now feel abandoned and forgotten.

The ongoing pastoral visit is the most demanding for the volunteer parishioner. This visit requires an awareness of the many emotional responses characteristic of the bereaved. It requires knowledge about grief along with patience and empathy. In order to train visitors, certain topics should be thoroughly discussed. The following breakdown of a three-session training program has been used effectively in a number of parishes. These models are readily adaptable to particular parishes.

Session One: *Pastoral Aims*

The introductory session focuses on the visitor's ministry. This first meeting initiates the parishioner to some bereavement symptoms. While the symptoms are important, the pastoral response is the primary concern.

The pastoral response to the death of a parishioner is the visit. A description of what a pastoral visit should consist of may be presented. A pastoral visit has the following aims:

1. The visitor is present to comfort and console. As a consoler there is a ministry of presence. It is being comfortable with silences.

2. The visitor encourages the bereaved to express their grief. He or she has to have good listening skills. The pastoral visitor thus helps the bereaved sort out feelings.

3. Empathy understood as putting ourselves in another person's position is essential. This means sharing the pain with the bereaved.

4. Help the bereaved find meaning. The pastoral presence reminds the bereaved of the religious context. This helps them to accept and cope with the loss.

5. The pastoral visitor has to assess how the grieving person is managing the grief. If there appear to be complications, the visitor should make this known to the priest or parish staff member. Training should focus on determining when to discuss a referral to a mental health professional.

The first session provides the pastoral visitor with an overview of the visit. A good reference work for this first session could be Rabbi Kushner's book, *When Bad Things Happen To Good People.*

Session Two: *Some Needs Facing The Bereaved*

In his work *The Minister as Crisis Counselor*, David K. Switzer outlines some of the apparent needs facing the grief-stricken. He positions grief ministry within the context of crisis resolution. The following points illustrate this:

1. Expressing and identifying feelings: such feelings of empti-ness, abandonment, yearning, anger, fear, and guilt have to be verbalized. In so doing catharsis may happen.

2. Reaffirming one's self: grieving is often accompanied by feeling of lowered self-esteem or worth. The selfhood has been disrupted by the loss of a significant other.

3. Severing or breaking an effective tie: this means letting go of the relationship with the deceased. Death necessitates this type of change. It is not insensitive to hope to accomplish this, as it helps to redefine our relationship with loved ones now that they have died. There is a process of forgetting or letting go and at the same time remembering other aspects about the loved one. It is a difficult balance to acquire. This heightens the need to have someone to talk to about the loss.

4. Recalling/remembering the deceased within one's self: re-membering is important to redefine the relationship with the deceased. Inasmuch as there was an intimate union, the presence of the other is still internalized. There is a need for the bereaved to be heard as they recall memories. This need can be very taxing on others. The visitor has to have patience as the bereaved recall and remember. The visitor, by listening carefully, helps the bereaved to slowly move on.

5. The need for interpersonal sharing. The bereaved have to direct their feelings outward. This is very problematic in a culture that does not give much opportunity to the bereaved to share feelings after the initial loss. This illustrates the importance of the pastoral visitor's role.

6. Rediscovering meaning: this need concerns how the bereaved relates to self, the deceased, the community, and especially God. The previous needs lead to the necessity of rediscovering what life means now that this loss has happened. Pastoral care is a vital source for empowering and resolving the loss.

There are specific theological difficulties which may be phrased as questions at this session. According to our appreciation of the needs, the following may be asked: Are the bereaved able to express emotions such as anger felt toward God or others? Does the liturgy help in expressing emotions? What can the parish do to help resolve the crisis of meaning facing the bereaved?

Third Session: *Points To Remember While Visiting*

This session may consist of some role-playing. It may be best for the pastoral leaders to take the part of the bereaved. After the role-playing, some small group discussion with reporting is advantageous.

The session may entail talking about support among the pastoral visitors. The pastoral visitor should be encouraged to keep confidential notes about his/her feelings before and after the visit. This helps to appreciate how growth or blocks to grief occur.

Some scheduling for future meetings and reflection sessions may be discussed. It is important for this ministry as well as others that the group meet regularly. Community building along with mutual support insures more fruitful results.

An overall checklist may be developed by the group. The following is a model which may be used:

1. Don't be afraid to touch or embrace the bereaved. Comfort happens with human contact.

2. Offer to help with activities of daily life. This includes everything from shopping to baby sitting.

3. Reassure the bereaved. Help them to face the loss. You may mention a hospital or parish support group.

4. Help them to put the loss into the wider context of religious meaning. You may accompany them to parish liturgies.

5. Become more familiar with the process of grieving.

6. Avoid platitudes at all costs. Platitudes are not pastoral care.

7. Permit the bereaved to express feelings of anger, abandonment, guilt, yearning to be with the deceased. Don't try to control the visit or the bereaved.

It is critical during the weeks and months following the funeral that we provide support for the bereaved. The ongoing need for pastoral care can only really happen when the community responds. Pastoral visitors embrace many aspects of ministry in caring and reaching out. They truly express the parish as the Body of Christ.

5.

The Funeral Homily As Pastoral Care

Changes in rituals affect every aspect of worship. The new *Order of Christian Funerals* clearly presents options which make a difference for people's grief. The new Order offers times during the rite of Christian burial which provide healing and hope for the bereaved.

The funeral ritual takes place at a moment of intense anxiety. The more the pastoral leadership is aware of the congregation's needs, the greater the possibility of healing. How the ritual fits in the pastoral setting is critical for its effectiveness. It must not be seen as merely a new book with rubrical changes. It is much more. It is a new clear call to action for the community.

The new ritual celebrates the deceased Christian's final journey toward the Kingdom. In the ritual some new stations or liturgical moments are added for prayer. These intense moments are: prayers at the time of death, gathering together when first in the presence of the deceased, the Vigil, the procession to the Church, and the final prayers of committal. These moments are opportunities for the bereaved to place the loss of the loved one into the wider context of religius faith.

The metaphor of journey provides us with rich insights and themes for funeral liturgies. Our words and gestures express

- 23 -

how we respond to the loss. The new ritual is sensitive to the theological importance of praying for the deceased Christian and also for the bereaved. The needs of the bereaved are highlighted so that those left behind can learn ways to begin to cope and refocus their lives in the face of their loss.

The homilist at the Vigil or the Funeral Mass in many ways sets the tone for the ritual's pastoral care and for the grief work to follow in the weeks and months after the loss. He is the key figure in determining how well the bereaved will journey with the deceased Christian. The homilist is the proclaimer and exclaimer of the scriptural messages of hope. In doing this he is also a pastoral caregiver. It is essential that homilitic themes be related to the pastoral psychology of the community of faith hearing the homily. Critical communal themes may be explored and presented which will directly affect the way the congregation grieves.

CRITICAL MOMENT

The funeral is a ritual of separation. It differs in intensity from all other rituals of transition in our life span. Letting go of a physical relationship is one of the most painful aspects of living. It is a crisis which cries out for companionship and consolation. The suffering of severing a bond of love requires support.

Christian community members acting as consolers is a critical theme for grief management. The bereaved need to hear that we need one another. It is in the context of community that the homilist helps the family and friends express their grief.

> In planning and carrying out the funeral rites the pastor and all other ministers should keep in mind the life of the deceased and the circumstances of death. They should also take into consideration the spiritual and psychological needs of the family and friends of the deceased to express grief and their sense of loss, to accept the reality of death, and to comfort one another.
>
> (para. 16) *Order of Christian Funerals*

When the meaning of community is proclaimed, the bereaved are made aware of a faith context for their expressions of sorrow. Their loss is not solitary. The community is not just there for an hour or two. The community suffers the loss with the bereaved, and will aid them through the times ahead. This is in keeping with St. Paul's theology of the Body of Christ. The homily is the time to stress how the visible Church connects with the Communion of Saints. This is a way for the bereaved to begin the process of redefining their relationship with the deceased.

Individualism is contradictory to healing for the grief-stricken. It only leads toward complications in adjusting to the loss. It limits expression and consolation which is so necessary in managing grief. Our culture tends to ignore, deny, or be indifferent to the needs of those who are grieving. The community, if it is to be truly Christian, must unify in the face of this fast death culture where grief work is limited to a quick church stop.

CRITICAL INSIGHTS

Crisis ministry assists people when they are experiencing transitions or losses. After the tragic Coconut Grove nightclub fire in Boston, studies were made of the survivors and victims' families. Those studies give us insights into the reactions people experience in crises and grief. While the Coconut Grove was a spectacular crisis involving great loss of life, that same critical experience is experienced by those touched by death. The death of a loved one puts a person into crisis just as real as the great human tragedies we read and see in the media.

The studies help both pastoral and secular caregivers to comfort the bereaved. When we know how to manage grief in the parish setting, very beneficial results occur.

SIGNICANT PASTORAL THEMES

The parish is the best possible setting for helping the bereaved acquire a sense of meaning regarding the death of a loved one. Pastoral care draws on scriptural concepts which relate to grief. When we see scripture and pastoral psychology complementing each other, our funeral homilies are very effective.

Preparing the funeral homily differs from all others. Keeping in mind some insights from "crisis ministry" can be very helpful. Some of the ways to intervene and assist the bereaved are (1) help the persons gain an understanding of the crisis, (2) assist them in accepting the reality, (3) help them to explore ways to cope, and (4) assist them in finding meaning in life.

Pastoral themes need to be grounded in Scripture. The Word expresses and heals at critical moments. Use themes which relate to the needs of the bereaved.

1. One theme to be stressed at the funeral rites is the journey of the deceased and the bereaved. The homilist can explain how the deceased's journey began at Baptism. They were carried into the Christian community as an infant. Now they are carried once again into the assembly of faith. This homily cites the symbols and rituals as they complement each other. The baptismal white garment is recalled in the funeral pall. The holy water once again reminds us of the deceased's Christian identity.

Some suggested scriptural readings for the funeral Mass are Genesis 12:1-4; Psalm 23; Hebrews 11:1-2, 8-10, 13-16; and John 6:44-51.

2. The covenant community which consoles is another significant theme for funerals. The covenant illustrates how the Christian bonds with others. Death is the severing of the bond or affectional tie. The funeral is the reestablishing of a new covenant relationship with our loved one who goes before

us in faith. Catholic theology complements the idea of covenant very effectively through our belief in our bond with the Communion of Saints. When covenantal theology is proclaimed, the homilist helps the community to realize the relationships with God and among themselves.

The Covenant as a community and biblical concept helps us to see a basis for the ministry of consolation. We realize our connectedness due to a spiritual bond. Some suggested scriptural references are Jeremiah 31:31-34; Psalm 23; 2 Corinthians 3:6; and Luke 22:20.

3. Another theme is that of seeking for life eternal. This relates to one of the most pronounced needs of the bereaved. Yearning or hungering to be with the loved one is a normal and yet intense feeling when we grieve. The homilist can assist the bereaved in identifying this feeling. It is important to know that the yearning is normal and can be put into the wider context of religious faith. We yearn and hunger for the Kingdom. Our hope informs our desire to be with our deceased loved one.

Some suggested readings for the funeral Mass are Isaiah 9:2, 6; Psalm 41 (42); 1 Corinthians 15:50-58; and John 6:44-51. This Gospel reading highlights our need for food for the eternal Jerusalem. It is a powerful expression of empowering, originating at the Table of the Lord.

There are many pastoral themes which directly relate to the needs of the bereaved. The homily heals by helping the community to express the loss.

In light of crisis theory, there are certain realities which the homilist ought to keep in mind. Some of the following insights for the homily may be helpful. (1) Do not use euphemisms for death. Rather help the bereaved to be oriented to the death. (2) Reinforce that life changes for both the deceased and the bereaved. "Life is not taken away, it changes." (3) Proclaim ways to cope by encouraging the family and friends to be patient and present to each other. The necessity to remember and ritualize the death may be mentioned. This may be done by encouraging the family to pray together, and especially to come together for Mass. (4) Encourage the family to be patient and present to each other as they grieve. If the members of the family are traveling, they should covenant to call frequently during this time and beyond. They should try to gather at significant family times to remember and reintegrate the deceased into their changed lives.

Emphasizing the funeral as separation is an intense psychological theme. Helping the bereaved to let go and mourn the loss is a releasing and healing aspect of liturgy. The funeral helps the bereaved to widen their perspective of loss. The Christian experiences it as the loss of a member of the community in communion with the whole Body of Christ. The Communion of Saints is one with the believing and praying community.

The revised funeral ritual clearly helps us to be pastorally caring. When we realize more about separation and loss, we are able to communicate and proclaim far more effectively. Critical insights provide us with better homilies which have a real impact for healing grief.

6.

Saying Farewell At The Funeral Liturgy

The *Order of Christian Funerals* possesses a unique vision and pastoral sensitivity. It is a valuable resource for ministry to the bereaved.

During the funeral, the bereaved begin the process of grieving. The painful ways of learning how to let go have to be experienced. In the new ritual the text and its correlation to the ministry of consolation highlights ways people can be psychologically oriented to events. This is a vital aspect in celebrating liturgy with people who are numbed by the loss of a loved one. The funeral liturgy orients the bereaved during what is a period of shock and numbness. The prayers, gestures, symbols, ministry, and participation all contribute to acknowledge the reality of separation. At the same time this is done with the support of the worshipping community.

The ritual recommends that the family take an active part in liturgical preparation. The pastoral opinions and actions are in themselves ways of intervening with those in crisis. When the family members become participants rather than observers, they cooperate in addressing the loss. This allows them to move more switfly through the process of initial grief.

The final Farewell (cf. para. 227) is an emotionally charged moment in the funeral liturgy. It concludes the ceremony in the Church and is the time when separation is felt in an intense way by all. The liturgy's words bring home the finality of the loss:

> Before we go our separate ways, let us take leave of our brother/sister. May our farewell express our affection for him/her; may it ease our sadness and strengthen our hope. One day we shall joyfully greet him/her again when the love of Christ, which conquers all things, destroys even death itself.
>
> *Order of Christian Funerals* (para. 22)

Silence follows this invitation to pray. It is here that a personal farewell may be made. A family member or designated friend may offer words of comfort through some brief recollections. This remembering the deceased loved one is an essential aspect of grief, and is a healing ritual. It clearly is in accordance with the ritual's pastoral vision of caring for those who are mourning.

PREPARING THE GUIDE

Liturgical preparation within the new ritual is an integral part of ministry to the bereaved. When the priest or pastoral caregiver meets with the bereaved in preparation for the funeral and related rites, it is an intense and meaningful time. At that time the unity between pastoral care and liturgical celebration is evident. The pastoral caregiver as representative of the community, lends support and guidance to the bereaved for all the funeral choices, especially in regard to the recollection. This kind of pastoral activity is evangelization for the parish as well as for the bereaved. The caregiver completes the ring of concern. He/she leaves the greater community to minister to individuals and returns to the community with responses and prayers for the individual.

The recollections about the deceased have to be consistent with the liturgical tone set by the ritual. Whoever is designated to present the recollections needs assistance in preparing the text. There should be a written text, as this ensures that the very difficult task of remembering actually is carried out in a focused way. Not having a text creates the possibility of being overwhelmed by emotion.

FAMILY RECOLLECTIONS

The ministry of consolation is evident when the Christian's life and relationships are noted in the liturgical setting. It is a meaningful part of the liturgy when family and friends hear the remembrance.

Recollection is a way of putting the remembrances into the context of faith. The community gathered together in faith should be helped to remember: (1) that the selection of scriptural texts give us some definite theological themes which relate to the recollections; (2) the funeral rites are to remember the deceased Christian in his/her relationship with God as a member of the believing community; (3) the recollections should be supportive to the bereaved; (4) the recollections should deepen our faith in eternal life as Christians.

RECOLLECTION GUIDE

When assisting someone in writing a recollection for use during a funeral liturgy, you both should review the readings selected for the liturgy. The following guidelines are helpful in reviewing the recollection:

1. Statements about the deceased ought to reflect the deceased's relationship to God/family/community.

2. Do the statements tell of the Christian legacy left behind for others to learn from?

3. Are the statements helpful to the family and friends in this time of loss?

4. Do the statements help others put this person's life into the broader context of Christian faith — that while this is a personal loss it must be seen through the eyes of faith?

The guidelines are offered to further the ministry of consolation. Personal recollections help do grief work. It is necessary to remember and recognize our relationship with loved ones. This helps us to say good-bye, and at the same time we are redefining our relationship with the deceased. Eventually, we come to realize that we still have a spiritual bond with those who have gone before us in faith.

REMEMBERING THEMES

I have noted that certain scriptural themes are helpful when preparing the recollection. On one occasion I heard a presenter cite the Book of Proverbs at the funeral of a middled-aged married woman. It was very moving to hear the friend use the Scriptures to recall and console the widower. Evidently the friend knew how happy the marriage had been, and used Proverbs to reflect that love. The following words were beautifully appropriate. The dead woman was very talented as a seamstress, and everyone in the family knew this about her. There was an expression of emotion as the words were read:

When one finds a worthy wife, her value is far beyond pearls. Her husband, entrusting his heart to her, has an unfailing prize. She brings him good, and not evil, all the days of her life. She obtains wool and flax and makes cloth with skillful hands. (Proverbs 31:10-14)

The words remembered about this deceased Christian friend, wife, and mother were placed in the context of faith. The conclusion of the presentation was prayerfully done in a scriptural way. "Give her a reward of her labors, and let her works praise her at the city gates." (Proverbs 31:31). The recollection in this instance was very much a prayer being offered by a friend during the liturgy.

Other scriptural themes relating to the deceased Christian may be explored during liturgy preparation. Characteristics about the deceased which are consistent with a Christian way of life may be noted, such as their commitment to family and the Church, the community, and religious faith. The Old Testament readings, the Psalms, and certainly the Gospel readings may be associated with the remembrance.

AVOID IDEALIZING

One caveat really ought to be observed. The presenter and pastoral caregiver have to avoid "idealizing" the deceased. We must avoid attributing statements or characteristics which just are not correct or true. I've heard on occasion a friend relate how the deceased struggled with difficulties. Mention was made about the deceased's addictions. At the same time it was noted that he received help from others and lived a meaningful life. The presenter did not avoid or overlook the deceased's whole life. This mentioning of difficulties illustrates the life of grace as it is operative in our lives.

What ought to be emphasized is the deceased's relationships in life as expressions of faith, hope, and love. The ability to live a virtuous life is a gift from God. Consequently, the remembrance is not a time for extolling the person's life or giving a eulogy. It is a time to make known that God is present in all we say and do. We live and breathe and have our being grounded in God's creative presence.

The following remembrance is a model which has been used. It helps those who prepare to read over what others have presented. It is no easy task to present for a family remembrances about a deceased loved one. However, it is rewarding to hear and witness the consoling ministry occurring during the liturgy.

REMEMBRANCE

When my mother-in-law asked me to do a recollection of _____, I was honored.

In my ten years as a member of his family I learned much from him. He taught me how to be the heart of a family. In his own quiet way he showed me what it really means to be a Christian. I never recall his making an unkind remark to anyone or about anyone except for the occasional politician who was breaking faith with people and hurting the less fortunate. _____ was always helpful to everyone — again and again I saw him go out of his way to help a relative, a friend or neighbor. Even during his many hospitalizations he always made time for people, he always had a kind word for everyone. People with problems sought him out for advice. While he didn't have a bunch of degrees, he had something more important — he truly cared for people — he put his faith into action. When people went to him with problems, I among them, he didn't condemm them or tell them what they should do. He heard them out and somehow after talking to him for awhile they had the right answer themselves.

When I think back on what _____ left us, not in terms of money or property, but in terms of what will really stay with us, I think of all the laughter and tears he shed with us. He was an open, emotional person who could be that way because he never lost the open lovingness we all had as children.

He trusted people and they trusted him. He loved people and they loved him. He believed in God and God believed in him, making him able to share and teach that love to his wife, his children, and grandchildren.

While _____ goes physically from us today and we cry — we miss him — his spiritual legacy of love will remain. We had his trust and his love — it is up to us to keep faith with God and him by continuing to love and support one another.

I'd like to end this recollection by sharing a prayer _____ gave to me when I was grieving the loss of my father. He told me it had helped him through tough times. It's a prayer we all know, but when he gave it to me it took a whole new meaning for me. I think it was his model for living.

PRAYER OF ST. FRANCIS

Lord, make me an instrument of your peace.
Where there is hatred, let me sow love,
Where there is injury, pardon,
Where there is doubt, faith,
Where there is despair, hope,
Where there is darkness, light,
And where there is sadness, joy.

O Divine Master, grant that I may not
*   so much seek to be consoled as to console;*
To be understood as to understand.

To be loved as to love;
For it is in giving that we receive—
It is in pardoning that we are pardoned;
And it is in dying that we are born to eternal life.

St. Francis of Assisi

It is not uncommon for family members to ask for a copy of the recollection. This request confirms the importance it has for the family. The recollection helps the bereaved to remember the funeral and what was said and done for the deceased Christian.

Including the option for recollection and saying good bye in this way is a real act of compassion. The ministry and participation intended by the new ritual is accomplished when the remembrance is done. It is a remembering which is sensitive to the needs of the bereaved. At the same time, it is a way of praying and placing the deceased's life into the context of faith. This is a necessary aspect of grief work which has to be done by all those who loved the deceased Christian in life. Now, the important task of remembering and relating to the deceased in eternal life has to be undertaken. The new ritual empowers us to do this as a worshiping community.

7.

Psalms For Separation And Loss

Pastoral care continually faces the challenge of helping others to find the more encompassing religious context for life's crises. The crisis of separation and loss cries out for religious expression.

The Psalms are a powerful resource for pastoral care. Both priest and parishioner can journey into the Psalms and find meaning and management of their grief.

Ministry to the bereaved brings a dimension for the grief-stricken not found anywhere else. Anger, feelings of abandonment, guilt, yearning to be with the loved one, and crying out for meaning are emotions which stimulate the bereaved to seek help. Very often the bereaved become confused about expressing feelings in the religious setting. They may gravitate toward the parish and still avoid discussing the loss.

Many grieving people do not know how to tell the priest or pastoral caregiver about conflicts. This is common when the grieving person is angry toward God for taking the deceased loved one. Somehow the bereaved misinterpret crying out as a lack of faith. The Psalms are a pastoral way to allow the bereaved to express their true feelings.

While the Psalms offer a richness of expression for the

assembly they also speak to individual's wants, needs, and hurts. By praying or even reciting the Psalms on an individual basis, the mourner can focus on feelings that need to be unlocked. This acknowledgment of our feelings of frustration and loss can lead us to the wider reality of God's abiding love (*hesed*) ever present while we are expressing hurt and pain.

REBUILDING TRUST

We can describe the bereaved's personality sometimes as lacking in confidence or trust. Losses often necessitate rebuilding the lost trust or faith in life. When significant loss occurs, every aspect of life shatters. There is total disorganization and chaos. Relating to the bereaved entails helping them to piece together their broken lives. This requires patience, presence, and empathy in a process which for many goes on for years. There really is no time limit for grieving.

> Helen, who is eighty-four years old, recently lost her forty-one-year-old daughter. The daughter died with no warning from an aneurysm. Helen had always been a very devout Catholic. Now, she has withdrawn and tells only a select few friends how she really feels. She is angry with God and feels abandoned. She feels guilty about her feelings.

The Psalms can be of considerable assistance while making a pastoral visit with Helen. You can see the look of relief come over grieving people when certain Psalms are prayed with them.

Psalm 130 touches many feelings affecting the bereaved. It also gives permission to express uncomfortable feelings "locked" away for fear of showing the death of faith. Reading and reflecting on Psalm 130 with Helen, we could well expect her to become relieved that her feelings of anger at God are normal. They may be seen as even appropriate for her loss.

PSALM 130

Out of the depths I cry to you, O Lord;
  Lord, hear my voice!
Let your ears be attentive
  to my voice in supplication:
If you, O Lord, mark iniquities,
  Lord, who can stand?
But with you is forgiveness,
  that you may be revered.
I trust in the Lord;
  my soul trusts in his word.
My soul waits for the Lord
  more than sentinels wait for the dawn.
More than sentinels wait for the dawn,
  let Israel wait for the Lord,
For with the Lord is kindness
  and with him is plenteous redemption;
and we will redeem Israel
  from all their iniquities.

There are other Psalms which are appropriate for parish ministry to the bereaved. Everyone is familiar with Psalm 23. This Psalm does set the tone for accepting the reality of loss. Amidst the loss there is need for guidance "through the dark valley." The metaphor of the Lord as our Shepherd is helpful especially when we feel directionless and confused.

Channeling the anger which is an expression of grief is no easy task associated with "grief work." We need to know of ways to let go and at the same time accept our feelings in an honest way. Here again we turn to the Psalms to process our feelings in a purposeful manner. Some highlights from the following Psalm relate to anger.

PSALM 22

My God, my God, why have you forsaken me,
    far from my prayer, from the words of my cry?
O my God, I cry out by day, and you answer not;
    by night, and there is no relief for me.

As this Psalm progresses there is a change of mood and a seeking of strength. There is the rekindling of trust. This is a channeling of the anger by actually conversing or even yelling at God.

Be not far from me, for I am in distress;
    be near, for I have no one to help me.

Identifying with the Psalmist's anger, feelings of loss, and crying out connects the bereaved with religious reality. It opens up and gives permission for them to be authentic in owning their feelings. At the same time these feelings are not thought to be immoral or abnormal. They are an entirely understandable human response to loss, something that has to be gone through with the hope of being able to take the risk of trusting and loving again.

The pastoral minister or caregiver who prays with the bereaved has to do some anticipatory grief work. Being prepared for the emotional response or lack of reaction is helpful. Other Psalms help the pastoral caregiver when praying with people trying to identify their feelings.

WHEN GRIEF IS LONGING

One of the most prevalent feelings associated with loss is longing to be with the loved one. Certain Psalms relate to this and help the bereaved to be aware of this normal feeling. (cf. Psalms 42, 63, 84, 143). The searching and longing for the loved one is expressed in the religious context.

PSALM 42

As the deer longs for the running waters,
*   so my soul longs for you, O God.*
Athirst is my soul for God, the Living God.
*   When shall I go and behold the face of God?*
My tears are my food day and night,
*   as they say to me day after day,*
"Where is your God?"

The final part of the Psalm shows the renewed trust in God. This takes time for the bereaved to experience. The Psalms remind us that we will not always be so downcast in the future. It may be advantageous for the pastoral caregiver to read only the parts of the Psalm that speak to the bereaved's feelings. Leaving a copy of the complete Psalm looks forward to when the whole Psalm speaks to the bereaved.

Why are you so downcast, O my soul?
Why do you sigh within me?
Hope in God! For I shall again be thanking you,
*   in the presence of my savior and my God.*

BEING A SHEPHERD

Those who are experiencing separation and loss need shepherding. The pastoral caregiver is a significant person for the bereaved. We shepherd according to the Twenty-Third Psalm when we walk with the bereaved through the valley of darkness, when we are present in the lives of those who are suffering. Our guidance entails helping the bereaved to chart a course through grief.

The reassurance and comfort provided by praying the Psalms can't be overstated. Pastoral care has to be rooted in the

Scriptures. The use of the Psalms in caring for the bereaved is a guidance provided by the word of God. It is revelation unfolding in front of us, evident as the grief-stricken gain insight, are revealed moments of grace, and dialogue with God.

When we keep the ministry of consolation in mind, our praying the Psalms takes on greater meaning. Certainly, deeper insights about ways to care for the bereaved will be given to us as we pray. The richness of meaning, hope and trust provided even as we lament changes not only our ministry but ourselves.

The Psalms for separation and loss are many. Our pastoral visits and care are assisted by the word of God with us. This provides us with more confidence and hope in ministry. When we pray the Psalms with others, the ministry is enkindled with Jesus' presence. This is a way of realizing the promise that we will not be abandoned or left orphans to rage against the darkness without hope.

8.

Music Expressing Pastoral Care

The new *Order of Christian Funerals* highlights the fact that "Music is integral to the funeral rites" (para. 30).

The funeral ritual addresses: (1) why it is important to have music; (2) what parts should always be sung: and (3) who is involved in singing (the whole community, and ministers of music, especially the cantor).

In the new ritual there is a vision for pastoral care which complements liturgical actions. This is consistent with the ritual's emphasis on ministry and participation. Music plays no small part in the ministry of consolation.

Music is a vital part of the funeral and grief experience. Through music we are able to appreciate the connection between liturgy and pastoral care.

Music is integral to the funeral rites. It allows the community to express convictions and feelings that words alone may fail to convey. It has the power to console and uplift the mourners and to strengthen the unity of the assembly in faith and love. The texts of the songs chosen for a particular celebration should express the paschal mystery of the Lord's suffering, death, and triumph over death and should be related to the readings from Scripture.   *(Order of Christian Funerals* (para. 30)

The ritual provides for music at liturgical moments or stations in the funeral rite. Music integrates the metaphor of the funeral as the Christian's final journey. Comforting music is a vital part of pastoral care and worship.

> Music should be provided for the vigil and funeral liturgy and, whenever possible, for the funeral processions and the rite of committal. The specific notes that preceded each of these rites suggest places in the rites where music is appropriate. Many musical settings used by the parish community during the liturgical year may be suitable for use at funerals. Efforts should be made to develop and expand the parish's repertoire for use at funerals.   *Order of Christian Funerals* (para. 32)

Selecting appropriate liturgical songs at funerals can make a difference in managing grief. The new ritual specifically spells out the importance of making correct selections.

> Since music can evoke strong feelings, the music for the celebration of the funeral rites should be chosen with great care. The music at funerals should support, console, and uplift the participants and should help to create in them a spirit of hope in Christ's victory over death and in the Christian's share in that victory.   *Order of Christian Funerals* (para. 31)

Liturgical music assists the bereaved to accept the reality of loss, redefines in a communal setting their relationship with the deceased, and helps them to receive insights to their own feelings of loss and ways to cope.

ACCEPTANCE OF LOSS

At the time of the funeral, many bereaved are still in a state of shock. There is a numbness to the reality that a loss has occurred. Accepting the fact that a loved one has died does not happen quickly. Many people need intervention to accept the reality of loss.

Intervention at this time occurs in a variety of ways. Ritual and music are vital in facilitating the grieving process. The bereaved are able to express feelings through the catalyst of music. Certain hymns remind the bereaved of times when they worshipped with the deceased loved one. This releases memories and emotions, and is a catharsis which is necessary and healing for mourners. It is a way of accepting that the loved one has died. Liturgical music opens up the floodgates and contributes to the managing and flow of grief. The bereaved should be encouraged to use "significant" hymns throughout the initial grief period and especially during the funeral rites.

It benefits the bereaved to participate in liturgical songs. A striking difference between liturgical and secular music is the religious context. Ritual and pastoral care help the bereaved put the sense of loss into the wider context of religious meaning.

One widow shared with the parish support group the impact music had on her grief. Often they start sessions with a hymn as the opening prayer. This helped her to recall how she felt.

"I didn't know my daughter had asked the soloist to sing *How Great Thou Art*. When the hymn began, memories came flooding back to me. I cried, yet I was happy about the wonderful memories. My husband loved that song and it was the best choice for music at the funeral."

LOSS AND THE COMMUNITY

The assembly unites in faith and love when a Christian dies. The burial of a Chirstian follows the metaphor of being the last procession or journey toward the Kingdom. The Pilgrim People of God process in song with the deceased loved one. This is powerfully expressed in the Old Testament when people sang Psalms as they ventured toward the Temple.

Liturgical music and song express community. Everyone including the bereaved worships together. This bonding and participation with the community assist the bereaved. Feelings of loneliness, withdrawal, isolation, and the "privatizing" of grief do not effectively resolve losses. By not addressing our brokenness, we only invite complications in our grieving. Such denial has had devastating results for the grief-stricken. Going through the grief entails accepting losses and working at reorganizing our lives. The parish as a communal setting is conducive to this need.

Many changes occur when a loved one dies. How different our lives become depends on the intensity of the bond with the deceased. This is what has been called intense grief and lesser grief reactions. Obviously, the closer we are to the loved one the more intense the grief. This relationship has to go through a process of redefinition, which is an integral part of effective grief work.

Liturgical songs can put our new relationship with the deceased into focus. If we look to the Psalms, we find enlightening ways to express our new relationship.

The Psalms are processional songs of praise. At various moments they play a vital role in the community's conversing with God. The prayers provide revelations about our human response to loss.

Selecting Psalms which help express the loss is very helpful. Parish liturgy and bereavement committees can research appropriate Psalms for funeral rites. The community and individual laments are a rich resource for worship and pastoral care for the bereaved.

The Psalms as sacred poetic songs remind the bereaved about trust in God. The Psalmist does this without denying our very human feelings of abandonment, emptiness, anger, and searching. Psalms 22 and 130 certainly reflect our deep feelings of loss. The Psalms guide us through the dark valley.

The Responsorial Psalms allow the community to respond with trust and express the loss. The ritual is sensitive to selecting Psalms which are appropriate for the needs of the mourners and the circumstances of the death.

The Liturgy of the Hours is another song celebration encouraged by the new ritual. cf. (*Order of Christian Funerals*, para. 348.) The entire community is invited to sing the Office for the deceased member of the parish.

Liturgical songs are meant to express the depth of the community's belief in eternal life and the resurrection of the dead.

AT THE FUNERAL

The opening song sets the tone of our belief as we gather together as a believing community. The moments of praise at the Gospel sung by the cantor again emphasize the resurrection. Other music, such as at the Preparation of Gifts, is meant to complement liturgical actions and provide a deep sense of reverence and meaning. This addresses a definite need facing the bereaved. The initial time of loss is one looking for meaning and trying to sort things out about life.

The Song of Farewell is the climax of the rite of final commendation. It is a moment when we affirm our trust and hope in the resurrection. This is a time for the family, friends, and fellow parishioners to "let go." The difficulties we encounter in separating are made meaningful by this song.

There are many hymns which evoke a faith response when we journey in that final procession with a deceased member of the Body of Christ. Some hymns certainly illustrate better than others the reality of combining Scripture, worship, and pastoral care. It has been noted how important it is for parish worship committees and bereavement committees to research and develop a repertoire of well-sung liturgical songs.

The hymn entitled "Be Not Afraid" by Bob Dufford, S.J., combines liturgy and pastoral care. The hymn serves as a model for developing music which contributes to helping the bereaved go through grief. The hymn helps us to place our loss into the wider context of religious meaning.

> *Refrain:* Be not afraid I go before you always. Come follow
> me and I will give you rest.

> 1. *You shall cross the barren desert,*
>   *but you shall not die of thirst.*
>   *You shall wander far in safety*
>   *though you do not know the way.*
>   *You shall speak your words in foreign lands*
>   *and all will understand.*
>   *You shall see the face of God and live.*

The loss of a loved one for many is a "desert experience." However, it does not have to be the dark night of the soul. No matter what we encounter, there is still the presence of God. The grief-stricken need reassurance that there is meaning and purpose.

> 2. *If you pass through raging waters in the seas,*
>   *you shall not drown.*
>   *If you walk amid the burning flames,*
>   *you shall not be harmed.*
>   *If you stand before the pow'r of hell*
>   *and death is at your side,*
>   *know that I am with you through it all.*

In many ways the death of a loved one is an experience in chaos. The biblical imagery in the song mirrors grief. This helps the bereaved to deal with the reality. At the same time, coping is put into the religious context. Our lives are dependent upon empowering from God. God is the one who guides us through the darkness and chaos. This verse is in keeping with the trust we find prevalent in the Psalms.

> 3. *Blessed are your poor,*
> *for the kingdom shall be theirs.*
> *Blest are you that weep and mourn,*
> *for one day you shall laugh.*
> *And if wicked tongues insult and hate you*
> *all because of me,*
> *blessed, blessed are you!*

This final verse and refrain offer a very significant reassurance for the bereaved. Early in grieving it is vital to know that our feelings will not remain the same. We are created not to sustain such painful emotions. We will with God's help feel better in the future. Often during the initial time of loss I find myself comforting others by letting them know this fact. Here again, like the Psalmist's words "You turned my mourning into dancing" the bereaved are provided consolation and hope in song.

Music brings comfort and consolation to the bereaved at a critical time. There are short and long term effects to songs during the funeral rites. The songs help us to express and accept our losses. What is most important is that this is done in the context of the Christian community. It is in this community that, despite our losses, we will be able to love again and be uplifted in song by the resurrectional presence of the Holy Spirit.

9.

Family Prayers During Bereavement And Beyond

Family Bibles have a section for recording baptism, weddings, and funerals. This is a tradition we don't want to lose in family life and history. The Bible offers much more than a place to record important events. During significant moments it is our source of strength, hope, and interpretation. This is especially telling when separation and loss occurs for the family.

Prayer services based on Scripture assist the family to place losses into the context of religious meaning. The *Order of Christian Funerals* is very pastoral and scripturally based.

At the time of death, the ritual recommends that the family come together for prayers. The model for prayer follows an outline of a reading from the Bible: a response, the Lord's Prayer, a prayer for the deceased person, a prayer for the mourners, and a blessing.

The prayer service consoles and at the same time begins for the mourners their journeying with the deceased loved one through the moments of Christian burial. For the next two or three days the entire family is brought together for the funeral. The family spends considerable time together.

During this time the ritual has moments for prayer (1) at the time of death, (2) at the gathering together for the first time at the funeral home, (3) at the Vigil Service or evening wake service, (4) in the morning when the family and friends are about to process to the Church, (5) at the funeral Mass, and at the cemetery. The purpose of these moments is to fill the time with prayer which consoles. The ritual allows through prayer the expression of feelings of loss.

The prayer services offered herein are intended to extend prayer among those who are grieving. The prayers may be adapted to meet the family's needs. They are a model to assist the family with accepting the reality that someone has died. At the same time, prayer services are meant to assist family members in coping. Grieving touches the whole family. However, there are many different relationships to the deceased. The grieving widow and the grieving daughter both in different ways are experiencing the loss. The prayer service opens up to the family members different ways of expressing the loss.

When a loved one dies, he or she is more present to us than perhaps any other time. We can vividly recall events which we thought were long forgotten. Somehow grieving means remembering in order to truly realize that our loved one has died. We need to sort out our feelings. This cannot be effectively accomplished without a support network. Usually the most immediate support network is our family.

Coming together in prayer with the family helps. Later when everyone goes home, the same prayer service is a reminder. In our minds we can identify with the daughter who took care of her mother. After mother's death she has to go home to an empty house. Special prayers even alone are a help in facing all the other losses which accompany death.

Connections among family members take place because of the gathering together in prayer. The prayers bring out the intensely personal feelings which have to be sorted out while grieving. At the same time there are definite psychological advantages. The ritual in the home assists the family in accepting that the loss really happened. The shock and numbness give way to a realization that the grief has to be expressed in different ways.

Some of the most prevalent needs facing the bereaved are addressed when praying is done with the family. It is a critical time when feelings of emptiness, yearning to be with the loved one, anger, fear, guilt, and abandonment have to be expressed. Family members can often provide the best care of all for the grieving spouse, sibling, or other close relative.

When we lose a loved one, part of ourselves dies. There is a lowering of self-esteem and self-worth. The gathering together reaffirms that we are still loved and lovable in our homes. Our feelings are validated by those who share the loss with us.

Another important aspect of loss is the breaking of an effective tie or bond. Our relationship with the deceased is drastically changed. There is a need to establish a new relationship. Our way of redefining though prayer brings purpose in a religious context of meaning.

The prayer service is a way of remembering and recalling the loved one's presence. In the psychology of grieving we have to go through the remembering if we are to let go. Grief work consists of a process of remembering and forgetting.

The initial time of loss is the introduction of grieving. The way the family mourns does make a difference. The following prayer services are designed to assist the family with mourning. They are meant to be a creative response to what is a shattering experience.

The prayer services are most effective when the family gathers together for preparing the liturgy. This may happen after the first viewing of the body. There is a need for the family to be strengthened in their journey through the rituals which take place on the day of the funeral.

FAMILY PRAYER SERVICE

Leader: God, come to our assistance.

Family: Lord, make haste to help us.

Opening Prayer

Leader: Lord, we gather together to remember our loved one _____ who has gone forth from us. Heal us as we pray for him/her as a family. Help us remember that we are journeying together toward the Kingdom of Heaven. This we ask in Jesus' name.

Family: Amen.

Leader: (or other designated reader)
A reading from the book of Psalms (Ps. 23)
The Lord is my Shephered. . . .

Leader: Let us close our eyes for a brief time and allow God to lead us through the darkness of this grief.

Petitions:

Leader: Let us now call upon God with the following petitions: It is painful for us to remember _____; help us to help each other in our pain, We pray to the Lord.

Family: Lord, hear our prayer.

Our love one _____ has been called out of this life. We ask you, Father, to grant _____ light, happiness, and peace. We pray to the Lord.

Family: Lord, hear our prayer.

Leader: Let us join hands and pray the prayer of the Kingdom. Our Father . . . .

Conclusion:

> *Leader:* Father, we thank you for bringing us together.
> Through your Son, Our Lord Jesus Christ, who
> suffered and died for us, come to our aid. Help us to
> prepare our final journey on earth with _____.
> Give us the hope and consolation of looking forward
> to the Heavenly reunion.   *Amen.*

The preceding prayer service is appropriate as the family
gathers during the initial time of grief. It may be adapted when
the family gathers for memorial Masses. Usually this happens
about a month after the funeral. This has been a custom for
many years in our culture. It is another one of those traditions
which for its wisdom we don't want to abandon.

The prayer of reflection before the Mass may follow with
some changes such as:

Opening Prayer:

> *Leader:* O loving God, we gather together once again as
> family to remember _____ who passed on to
> eternal life. We trust in your loving presence to
> embrace _____ with your kindness. Help us to
> continue with our life's journey with the consolation
> you give us through your Son and the working of the
> Holy Spirit. This we ask as a believing family.
>
> *Amen.*

There are other prayers which can comfort and bring
consolation to others at critical times after the death of a loved
one. Some of the significant times are anniversaries and holidays. Prayers within the context of the family gathering are very
consoling and contribute toward the family's well-being. An
appropriate introduction to a prayer service at the time of a
birthday is the following:

Introduction:

> *Leader:* O Lord, today we recall when _____ was born.
> We believe that he/she has now entered into eternal
> life. We ask you to console us and grant _____
> light, happiness, and peace in your Kingdom. This
> we ask in the name of your Son and in the Holy
> Spirit.

Amen.

Prayers in the home are meant to complement the prayer of the Christian community. One of the finest results of the new *Order of Christian Funerals* is the emphasis on communal praying. Morning and evening prayer are emphasized as part of the ritual. There are many options offered for a variety of prayers and intentions in this ritual (cf. para. 398-399). The Office for the Dead (Cf. para. 370) may also be celebrated in the home of the deceased.

We are truly the People of God when we gather together in prayer. The combining of many small gatherings into the gathering of the assembly is an important pastoral goal. The prayer life of the family experiencing loss can be a powerful expression of our Christian faith and the real meaning of the ministry of consolation.

Our prayers can be effective in confronting crises and receiving comfort. They assist us in finding meaningful ways to grieve. They allow us to go beyond ourselves and glean insights to the mystery of life, death, and resurrection.

10.

Ritualizing Our Losses

Caregivers are often at a loss when dealing with grief. Seeing and dealing with raw emotions puts the caregiver on the cutting edge of family rituals. These actions which families employ not only express their loss but begin to manage it in real terms.

We can think of rituals as vehicles which express symbolic social behavior. There are both private and public aspects. For the most part rituals are performed as a group. They often symbolize the group's identity. In the religious realm the importance of rituals can't be overstated. The ritual allows people to look into and beyond events to their deeper meaning.

As the pastoral caregiver builds rapport with families, it is noted that some families are better at ritualizing losses than others. For those not predisposed to rituals, encouragement has to be provided as they search for ways to express grief.

Very often the pastoral minister is the primary contact for the bereaved. The families need reassurance that they are "normal" in expressing themselves. The more aware the professional is about rituals, the better he/she can assist the grief-stricken.

Rituals are ways of expressing transitions in life. The phrase "rite of passage" was first used in 1909 by the French anthropologist Arnold van Gennep. Rituals were studied by him in the life cycle. Events such as childbirth, adolescence, death and other major occurrences were signified by rituals or set patterns of actions. These ceremonies helped people to acknowledge the passage from one state in life to another. In many ways rituals helped to redefine relationships and finalize changes.

Arnold van Gennep very carefully analysed a number of common life cycle changes. He grouped rituals under three main categories: preliminal, liminal, and post-liminal. The word "liminal" originates in the Latin "limen" meaning "threshold."

Life, according to the anthropologist, consists of a number of thresholds. The pre-liminal is the state of balance. This is followed by the liminal which is the state of crisis or crossing. The post-liminal is the time beyond or post-critical.

This provides us with a better understanding of funerals. We could easily think of the funeral as a ritual only for separation. However, it is more than that. It is the expressing of separation and loss. Rituals relate to the transition and reincorporation.

Separation is evident as there is a need to "let go." This is best done by individuals with others through common actions and gestures. It is a time to say our farewells.

The transition indicates a change from one state to another. This is clearly evident in weddings. There is the change of status from being single to married. Funerals similarly illustrate a change of status. When a spouse dies a person becomes a widow or widower. There are many other relationships we could cite as further examples. What is important to realize is that the ritual acknowledges the fact that everything is different. Not only is there a new relationship with the deceased but also in the entire family.

We have to be careful not to overlook the aspect of reincorporation. Not only do the mourners view the deceased in a different light, they see themselves as different yet connected to the community. There is in the ritual an including of the bereaved. This is very important in dealing with losses. This aspect shows how coping is possible with others. When we realize what rituals can accomplish, we can see their value.

At the same time we are more open to helping others to "ritualize." The pastoral caregiver often hears requests which are very important for families. These requests cannot be treated lightly. One example of a family ritual is when the funeral cortege goes by the deceased's home for the last time. This is a significant ritual action for the family and friends. It really does illustrate separation, transition, and a saying good bye to the loved one.

No ritual action is insignificant. The pastoral caregiver is involved in a request or action which has considerable meaning for a mourner. Somehow those rituals will stay with them throughout life.

Rituals take us through life's events. Not only do rituals play a vital role at funerals, they play a role in the grieving process. Our losses have to be creatively expressed.

Intense grief is like going into chaos. It is the opposite of creation which brings order and purpose out of life's emptiness. There can be a transition from chaos to creativity. This is where ritual is so very instrumental in managing grief.

Artists, writers, sculptors, and poets have given us many ways to ritualize. Accepting and managing grief is aided by rituals. Rituals are meant to release rather than control our emotions. Very often there is the mistaken opinion that self-control is reinforced by rituals. Nothing is further from the truth. The ritual is a way to help the bereaved to cope with the bereavement experience.

The readjustment which has to be done is often over-whelming for the bereaved. Rituals have a way of facilitating the adjustment. Certain rituals are necessary to sort out our feelings and allow us to accept the loss. One example is taking care of the deceased's belongings. In itself the distribution of the belongings is a ritual. When there is help provided by one or more family members, it becomes a ritual. The sorting out of clothing and other personal effects sorts out much more in our grieving.

You may want to make out a check list of ways to assist the bereaved in ritualizing. This would entail some of the following suggestions:

1. Make certain that there is sufficient explanation and encouragement for family participation in the funeral rites. In the new ritual such actions as putting on the funeral pall, selecting readings, bringing up the offertory gifts, suggesting a remembrance during the final farewell, and selecting music are very important.

2. Listen for special requests.

3. Place flowers on the casket in the cemetery.

4. Remember to stay in contact with the family if they have questions about grieving.

5. Act as a resource to help them ritualize or work out their grief. Sometimes this means referring them to a support group.

Sometimes we are more involved with rituals than we may think. This chapter has been meant to help us realize how ritual plays many parts in our lives. Everyday life is filled with social rituals. They are a real necessity for any society. When there is a crisis, the ritual really is a necessity. It does make a difference. Our lives can be more meaningful the more creative we are in responding to life's critical events through rituals.

11.

Developing A Theology
Of Bereavement

The *Order of Christian Funerals* highlights the importance of a ministry of consolation. This is a welcome innovation originating with the new ritual's vision for pastoral care. Yet, there is a need to develop a theology consistent with pastoral practices.

Theology and ministry working together correlate for the parish community a deep sense of meaning. A theology of bereavement opens up for the believing community ways of relating to God when we experience valleys of darkness.

We are a resurrectional people who celebrate life. At the same time, celebrating the resurrection sometimes takes considerable time for bereaved believers. A sound theological understanding helps us to do this.

This chapter explores our need to express life's losses and to do this according to Scripture, theology and pastoral psychology. The parish is the best of all possible settings for developing better ways to experience the mystery of God in the context of loss. It is grace which eventually converts our grief to gifts or charisms. These gifts are insights hitherto unknown in our lives.

PASTORAL PSYCHOLOGY AND GRIEF

Pastoral psychology provides us with insights regarding the grieving process. Our rituals are healing realities for the bereaved. It takes considerable time for the grief-stricken to orient themselves. This is especially true when the loss is sudden and unexpected. How we relate psychologically ought to be consistent with our pastoral theology.

Those suffering a loss are often numbed and shocked. (It is possible for any emotion to surface.) It is not uncommon for the bereaved to be angry at God or to feel abandoned by Him and the Church. How we respond to the flood of feelings overwhelming the bereaved is a psychological and theological challenge.

A defensive or apologetic posture does not do anyone any good. A celebrating or accepting attitude may not be appropriate for the bereaved during the initial phrase of loss.

Developing a theology for the bereaved involves wondering if we have allowed them to go through the process of grieving. We are indeed a hopeful people, but it takes time to accept our losses. Grieving precedes our organized and purposeful view of life.

Formerly, pastoral theology emphasized that we live in a "valley of tears." We may have let the pendulum swing too far with our celebrative stance. People need time and space to move toward being hopeful again. Sometimes the worst possible psychology is to be too quick to mention hope. Rebellion, anger, guilt, yearning to be with the loved one are entirely too operative in the bereaved's life when losses happen. It is a chaotic and confused time. Our pastoral concern is to help the bereaved sort and process emotions in order to go through the critical event.

REVELATION AND RESOLVING OUR LOSSES

Scripture relates to the complex human responses to loss. The human reaction and interaction with the mystery of God during bereavement deserves theological scrutiny. This theology includes the bereaved along with those who are care givers.

One of the strongest characteristics we may associate with grief is the need to redefine our relationship with the deceased, others, and God. During bereavement revealing or unveiling can happen both for the bereaved, care givers, and communities. Loss forces us to re-evaluate our interpretation of life and its ultimacy.

Biblical categories describe our relationship with God and one another. Reflecting on biblical symbols facilitates the need to redefine our relationship with supportive models. Bereavement can be placed into a wider context of meaning when we associate it with God's self-communication.

The concept of covenant is an all-inclusive model for a theology of bereavement. For us as for the Israelites, it is a concept through which we see all God's action. It colors all we do and all we are. No longer can we experience death as final. We see death not as taking away but rather as change, due to our being in covenant both individually and as community. It is God in the covenantal relationship who breaks the chains of bereavement.

It is God who is acting in a loving way to assist and be present to the Israelites. Amidst the experiences of separation and loss, there is the promise of fulfillment evident in this relationship. The Old Testament Covenant was for Israel the beginning of all religious thought. The covenantal relationship includes all the struggles, chaos, and loss. The image of God being with the people is experienced by ritualizing the covenant reality. The aspects of trust, fidelity, hope, and love are filtered through this experience. This theology is evident in the Psalter.

The poetic metaphors found in the Psalms address bereavement with the covenantal relationship. There are the many laments which we realize through the Psalmist's faith as expressions of loss. The loss is expressed within the wider context of the relationship with God. The covenant is the bond or effective tie which gives meaning to all of our relationships.

Theologizing about bereavement means recognizing that the Christian community is covenantal. There are bonds and effective ties among its members in the Body of Christ. According to St. Paul, when one member suffers all suffer.

The new ritual is conscious of our affectional ties to those who have died. In light of these ties, prayers are offered for the deceased.

> My brothers and sisters, we believe that all the ties of friendship and affection which knit us as one throughout our lives do not unravel with death. Confident that God always remembers the good we have done and forgives our sins, let us pray, asking God to gather _____ to himself.
>
> *Order of Christian Funerals* (para. 71.)

Redefining our relationship with those who have died ought to happen with the support of the covenantal community. We can cry out and even yell at God. God's love is mediated by other Christians' love.

CREATION AND BEREAVEMENT

Another important biblical concept which relates to grief is creation. The loss of a close relationship or bond is a shattering experience. the chaos and the void in a great abyss are biblical descriptions which apply to critical moments of loss. The experience of intense grief is manifested by disorganization. There is a need to be empowered and creatively proceed toward reorganizing our lives. The shared effort of ministry among the members of the community facilitating the managing of grief is an act of continual creation.

Ministering to the bereaved means cooperating with the creative power or grace. It is choosing life and helping those who experience death to pass from darkness to light.

The biblical reality of the wandering in the desert and searching for direction relates to grieving. The Israelite "desert experience" is the place where revelation occurred. Amidst existential emptiness, spiritual growth is possible.

THE NEW COVENANT AND CONSOLATION

The New Covenant is by its very nature communal. In the Eucharist there is the expression of fellowship or participation in the Spirit. The community becomes the agency by which the Spirit is operative in the world.

The Incarnational presence of Christ is continued in the community of faith. There is a continual creation especially in ways of bringing consolation to those experiencing losses. There has to be a sensitivity to the bereaved's needs. The community has to allow the grief-stricken to release their feelings of emptiness, anger, and abandonment. It is in the community that this is possible. Once there is the appreciation that all share a special convenantal relationship, real consolation is possible. The co-venant insures trust and openness. It allows for the loosening of a bond in due time.

The biblical perspective provides us with a theology for the bereaved. The Scriptures are the resource for the community. Our dialogue with God is deepened as we explore revelation, especially during our experiences of loss. Losses in the Christian community are times which are opportune for spiritual growth. They are times when we can open ourselves to ponder realities. Grief can be a graced moment for the bereaved. During that time of suffering and crying, there is still support. When others who share their faith reach out and care, the bereaved begin to see beyond the loss to the bright new hope — the eternal Jerusalem of the People of God.

Theology in the context of bereavement takes on a rich interpretation of what it means to have and to be a community of faith. The healing necessary to go through the darkness of grief is present among the community of believers. The more expansive concepts of life, covenant, creation, and healing are present for the bereaved.

Bereavement marks the time when we as mortals stand on the precipice of our worldly experience and glance into eternity. Not only do we experience crushing loss, we also begin to see there is more than just that. The limitations of seeing are corrected by our faith relationship with God. When we walk by faith, the horizon is limitless.

Bereavement theology seeks to harness the concepts and perspective woven throughout the experience of separation and loss. Once this is put into the wider context of Christian faith and covenant, comfort is possible. Developing a theology of bereavement entails interpreting life's losses in light of revelation. This . revelation allows us to appreciate our affectional ties among ourselves bonded together in the Body of Christ.

Bibliography

Abbot, Walter, and Joseph Gallagher. *The Documents of Vatican II.* New York: Guild Press, 1966.

Anderson, Bernhard. *Out of the Depths: the Psalms Speak for Us Today.* Philadelphia: the Westminster Press, 1983.

Boadt, Lawrence, Mary Dombeck, and H. Richard Rutherford. *The Rites of Death and Dying.* Collegeville, MN: the Liturgical Press, 1988.

Bruggeman, Walter. "From Hurt to Joy, From Death to Life," *Interpretation* XXVIII, no. 1 (January, 1974): 3-20.

Caplan, Gerald. *An Approach to Community Mental Health.* New York: Grune & Stratton, Inc., 1961.

Catholic Conference of Canadian Bishops. "The Christian Funeral," *National Bulletin on Liturgy* 22, no. 119 (December, 1989): 197-257.

Clinebell, Howard J. *Basic Types of Pastoral Care and Counseling: Resources for the Ministry of Healing & Growth.* Nashville: Abingdon Press, 1984.

Curley, Terence P. "Now Funeral Ritaul Means Change for Funeral Directors," *American Director.* Vol. 114, No. 3 (March, 1991): 24-26.

_____. "When the Community Laments," *The Priest.* Nov. Vol. 47, No. 6 (1991): 32-34.

_____. "Separation and Loss," *American Director.* Vol. 114, No. 11 (November, 1991) (36).

_____. "Psalms for Separation and Loss," *The Priest.* Nov. Vol. 47, No. 11 (1991) (41).

_____. "Establishing A Caring Group to Support the Bereaved," *Pastoral Life.* Vol. 40, No. 10 (November, 1991).

———. "Homelessness: Relating to the Grief," *The Priest*. Oct. Vol. 47, No. 10 (1991) (12).

———. "Music Expressing Pastoral Care for the Bereaved," *Pastoral Life* Vol. 41, No. 1 (January, 1992): 21-26.

———. *The New Order of Christian Funerals, Ways to Minister and Participate*. Kansas City, MO. Sheed & Ward, 1993.

Duffy, Regis. *A Roman Catholic Theology of Pastoral Care*. Philadelphia: Fortress Press, 1983.

Erikson, Erik H. *Toys and Reasons: Stages in the Ritualization of Experience*. New York: W.W. Norton & Co. Inc., 1977.

Greenberg, Ira A. *Psychodrama: Theory and Therapy*. New York: Behavioral Publications, 1974.

Grimes, Ronald L. *Beginnings in Ritual Studies*. Washington, D.C. University Press of America, 1982.

———. Ritual Studies, *The Encyclopedia of Religion*, 12:422-425, edited by Mircea Eliade. New York: MacMillan, 1987.

Grollman, Earl A. *Living When A Loved One Has Died*. Boston: Beacon Press, 1977.

Hoff, Lee Ann. *People In Crisis: Understanding and Helping*. Reading, MA: Addison-Wesley Publishing Company, 1984.

International Commission on English in the Liturgy. *Order of Christian Funerals*. Washington, D.C., 1989.

Jernigan, Homer. "Pastoral Care and the Crises of Life." In *Community Mental Health: the Role of Church and Temple*. ed. Howard Clinebell, Nashville: Abingdon Press, 1970.

Jewett, Claudia. *Helping Children Cope With Separation And Loss*. MA: Harvard Common Press, 1982.

Johnson, Sherry E. *After A Child Dies: Counseling Bereaved Families*. New York: Springer Publishing Company, 1987.

Jordan, Merle. *Taking on the gods: The task of the Pastoral Counselor*. Nashville: The Abingdon Press, 1986.

Kubler-Ross, Elizabeth. *On Death and Dying*. New York: MacMillan, 1969.

Kushner, Harold. *When Bad Things Happen To Good People*. New York: Avon Books, 1981.

Lewis, C.S. *A Grief Observed.* New York: Bantam Books, 1961.

Lindemann, Erich. "Symptomology and Management of Acute Grief," *American Journay of Psychiatry.* 101 (1944): 141-148.

McNiff, Shaun. *The Arts In Psychotherapy.* Springfield, IL: Charles C. Thomas Publisher, 1981.

Mitchell, Kenneth R. amd Herbert Anderson. *All Our Losses, All Our Griefs: Resources For Pastoral Care.* Philadelphia: The Westminster Press, 1983.

Parad, Howard J. *Crisis-Intervention: Selected Readings.* New York: Family Services Association of America, 1966.

Parkes, Colin Murray. *Bereavement Studies of Grief in Adult Life.* New York: International Universities Press, Inc., 1972.

Rando, Therese A. *Grief, Dying, And Death: Clinical Interventions For Caregivers.* Illinois: Research Press Co., 1984.

Robbins, Arthur. *Expressive Theraphy: A Creative Arts Approach to Depth-Oriented Treatment.* New York: Human Sciences Press, 1986.

Rutherford, Richard. *The Death of a Christian.* New York: Pueblo Publishing, 1980.

Seig, Thomas H. "Preaching at Funerals: Homily or Eulogy?" *The Priest* 40 (1984): 42-44.

Smith, Walter, S.J. *Dying in the Human Life Cycle.* New York: Holt, Rinehart, and Winston, 1985.

_____. *Aids: Living & Dying with Hope.* New York: Paulist Press, 1988.

Sofield, Loughlin, and Carol Juliano. *Collaborative Ministry: Skills and Guidelines.* Notre Dame: Ave Maria Press, 1987.

Sullender, R. Scott. *Grief and Growth: Pastoral Resources for Emotional and Spiritual Growth.* New York: Paulist Press, 1985.

Switzer, David. *The Minister As Crisis Counselor.* Nashville: Abingdon Press, 1974.

Turner, Victor. (ed.) *Celebration: Studies in Festivity and Ritual.* Washington, D.C.; Smithsonian Institute Press, 1982.

_____. "Ritual Tribal and Catholic." *Worship* 50 (6): 504-526.

van Gennep, Arnold. *the Rites of Passage.* translated by Monika B. Vizedom and Gabrielle L. Caffee. University of Chicago Press, 1960.

Viorst, Judith. *Necessary Losses.* New York: Ballantine Books, 1986.